THE ORIGINAL #2020 ADULT COLOURING BOOK

Fun and Stress Relieving Patterns incl.
Mandalas, Flowers, Animals and Many More

James Colouring Press

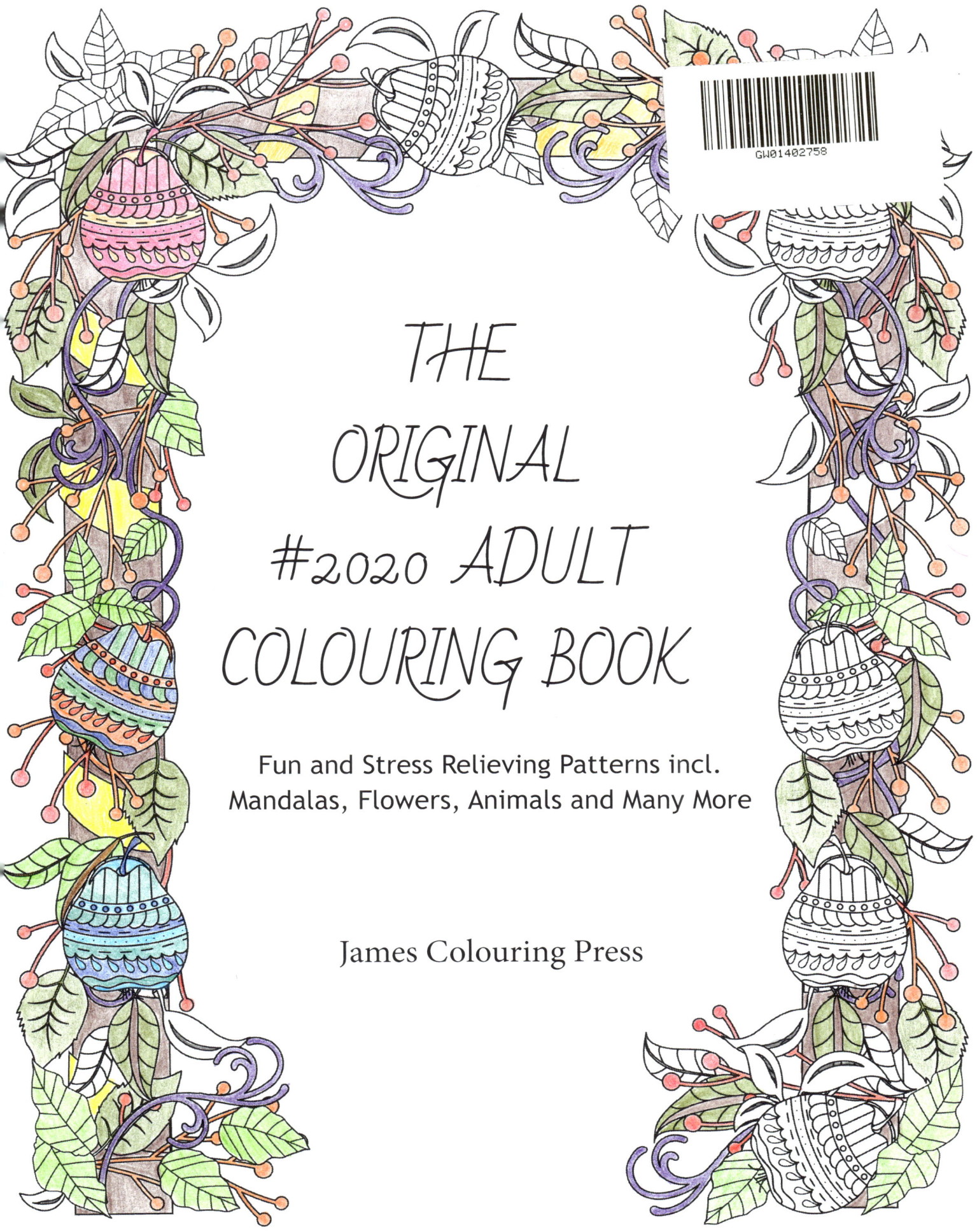

Various Stress Relieving Patterns incl. Animals, Mandalas, Flowers and Many More

- Various Levels Of Intricacy Keeping You Excited!
- Garden Designs, Animals and Mandalas Patterns
- Each Colouring Page Is Designed To Help Relax And Inspire
- Perfect For Every Skill Level And So Many Different Themes To Choose From
- Perfect With Your Choice Of Colouring Tools (Crayon, Gel Pens, Markers, Colored Pencils)
- High Resolution Crisp Clean Printing Of Illustrations
- Frequently Gifted. This Book Makes The Perfect Gift For Christmas Holidays, Birthday and More.
- Grab a Set of Pencils To Go With It!
- Create Your Own Frame-Worthy Masterpieces!

ANIMALS

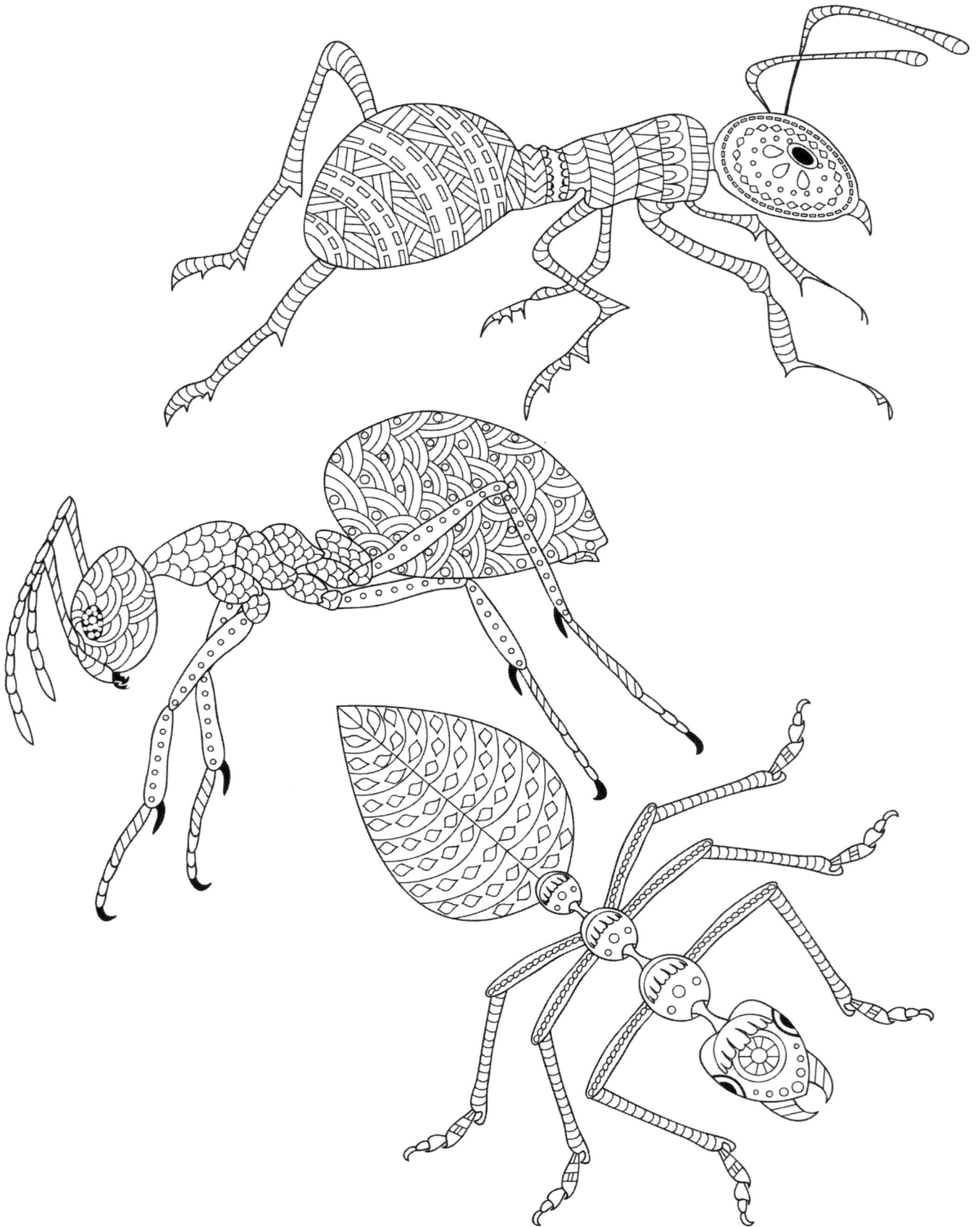

18

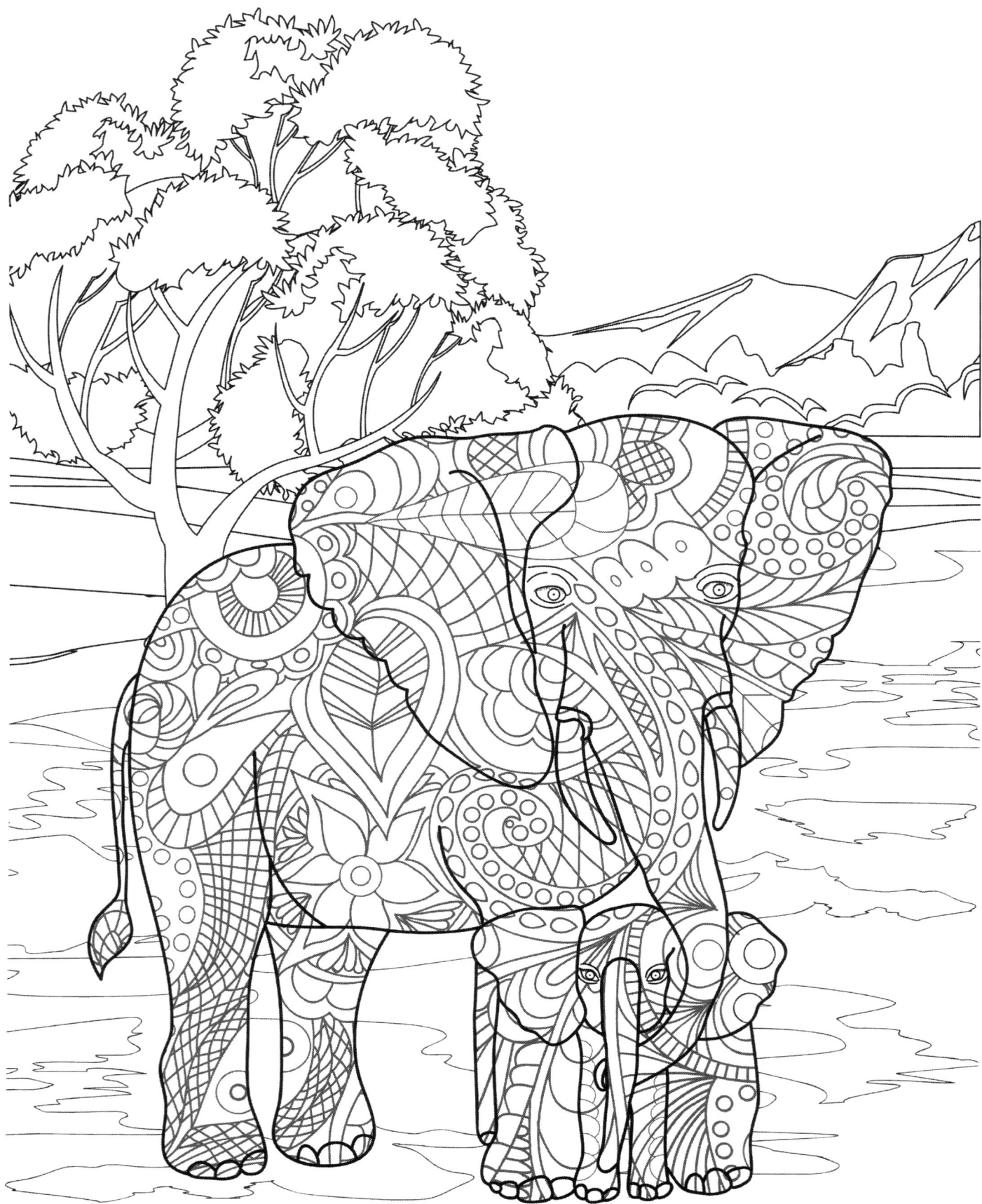

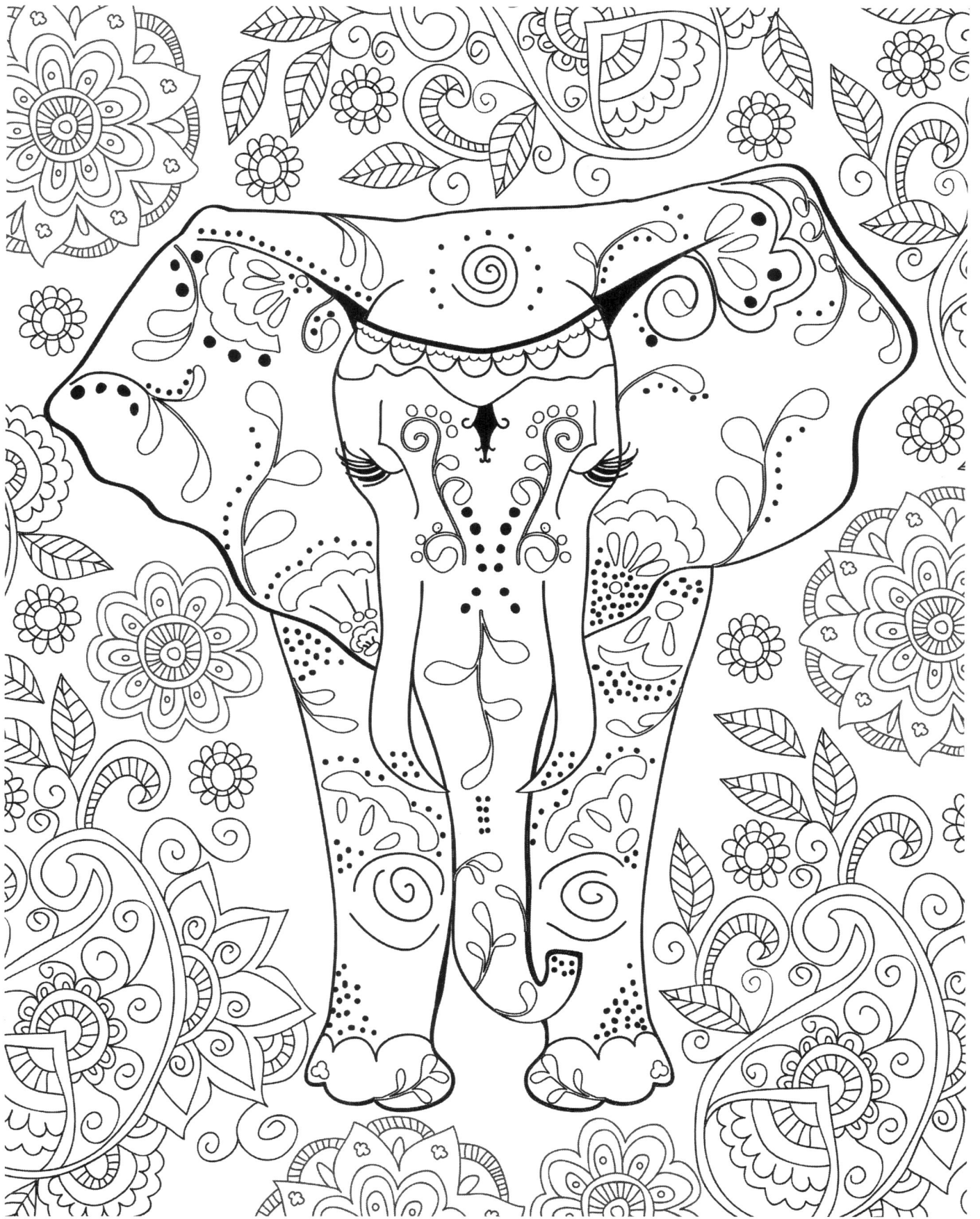

MANDALAS

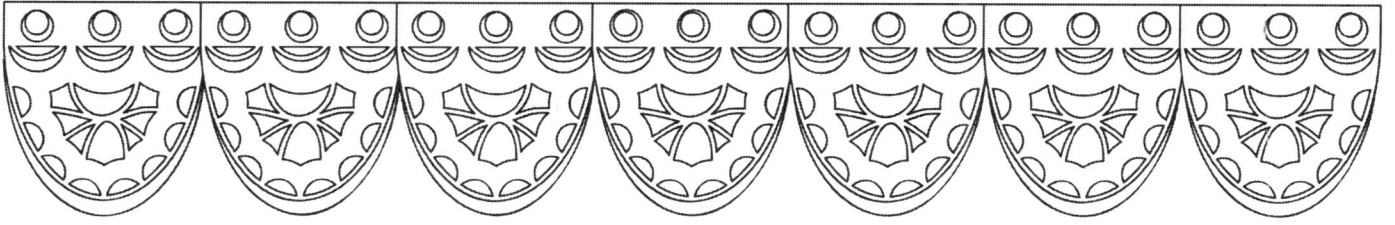

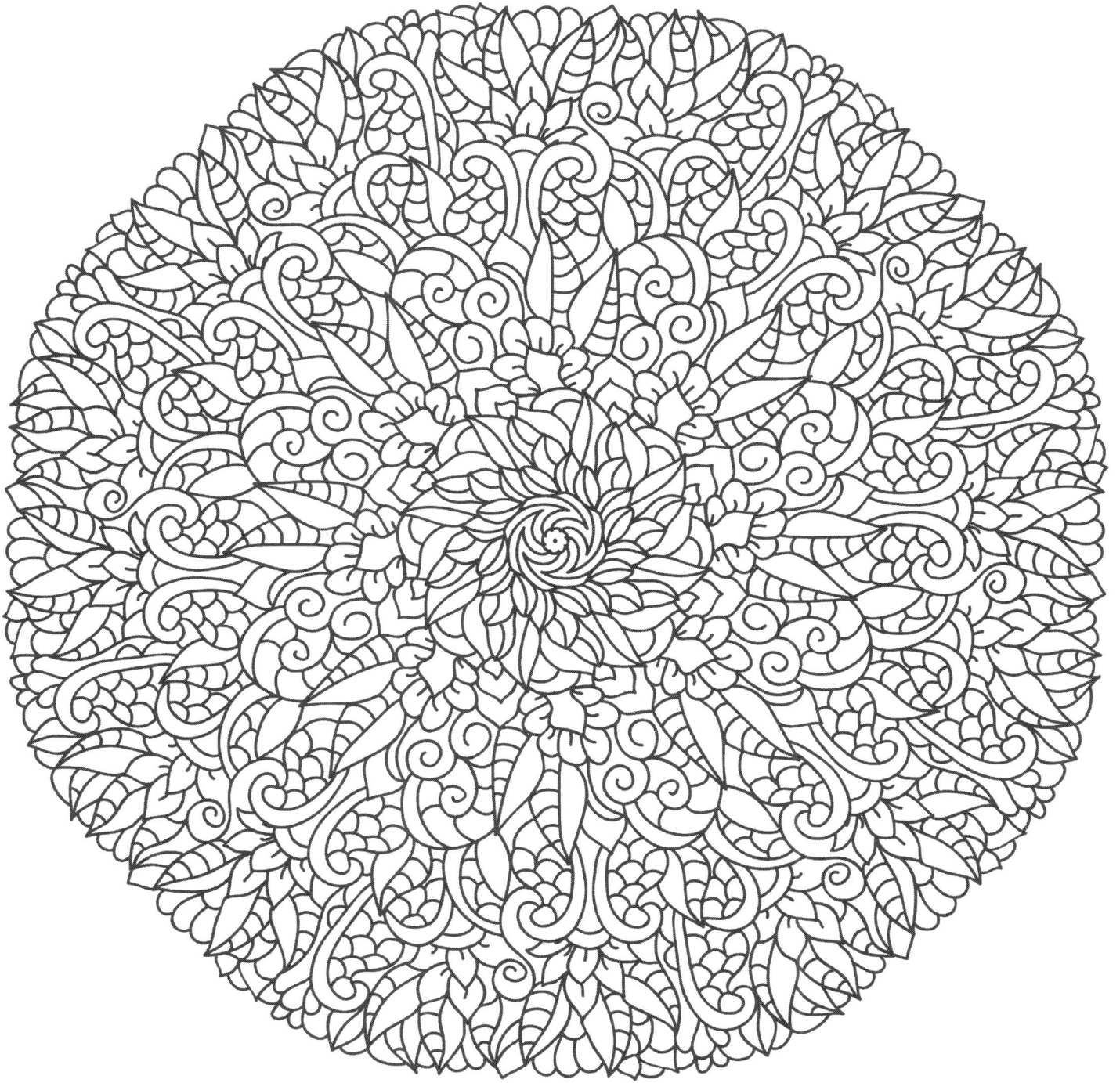

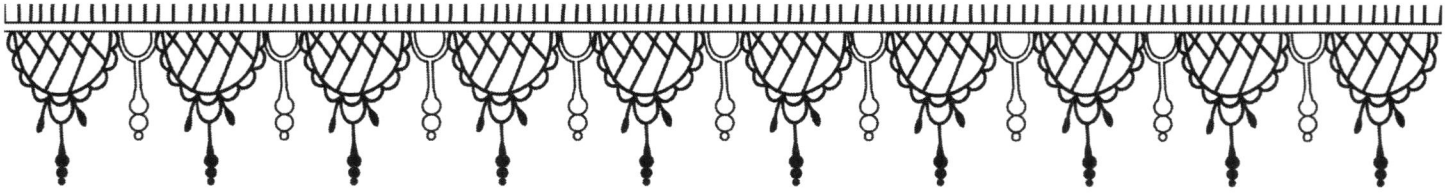

OTHER

PARIS

"You are the **LIGHT** of the world. A town built on a hill cannot be hidden.

--Matthew 5:14"

You prepare a table before me
in the presence of my enemies.
You anoint my head with oil.
My cup runs over.

Psalm 23:5

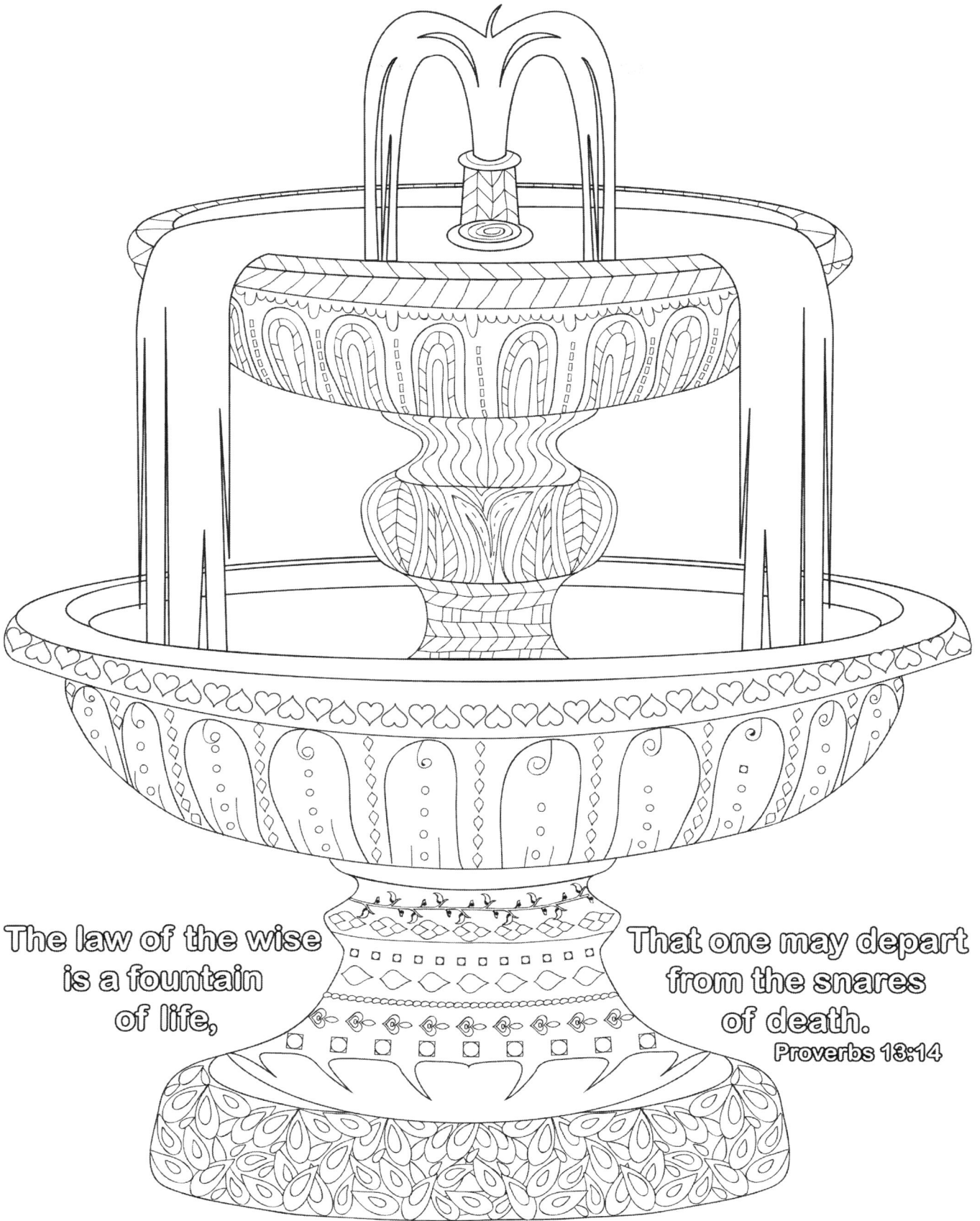

The law of the wise
is a fountain
of life,

That one may depart
from the snares
of death.
Proverbs 13:14

A word fitly spoken
is like apples of gold
in settings of silver.
Proverbs 25:11

DISCLAIMER

The opinions and ideas of the author contained in this publication are designed to educate the reader in an informative and helpful manner. While we accept that the instructions will not suit every reader, it is only to be expected that the recipes might not gel with everyone. Use the book responsibly and at your own risk. This work with all its contents, does not guarantee correctness, completion, quality or correctness of the provided information. Always check with your medical practitioner should you be unsure whether to follow a low carb eating plan. Misinformation or misprints cannot be completely eliminated. Human error is real!

Coverdesign: Natalia Design
All templates by Imagepluss // www.shutterstock.com

Printed in Germany
by Amazon Distribution
GmbH, Leipzig